WILL
SELF

SCALE

PENGUIN BOOKS

PENGUIN BOOKS

Published by the Penguin Group. Penguin Books Ltd, 27 Wrights Lane, London w8 5tz, England. Penguin Books USA Inc., 375 Hudson Street, New York, New York 10014, USA. Penguin Books Australia Ltd, Ringwood, Victoria, Australia. Penguin Books Canada Ltd, 10 Alcorn Avenue, Toronto, Ontario, Canada m4v 3b2. Penguin Books (NZ) Ltd, 182–190 Wairau Road, Auckland 10, New Zealand · Penguin Books Ltd, Registered Offices: Harmondsworth, Middlesex, England · *Scale* was originally published in a limited pictorial edition and subsequently in an abridged version in *Granta*. It appears in Will Self's collection of stories *Grey Area* (Bloomsbury, 1994). This edition published 1995 · Copyright © Will Self, 1993, 1994 · All rights reserved · The moral right of the author has been asserted · Typeset by Datix International Limited, Bungay, Suffolk. Printed in England by Clays Ltd, St Ives plc · Except in the United States of America,
10 9 8 7 6 5 4 3 2 1

Prologue

(to be spoken in conversational tones)

The philosopher Freddie Ayer was once asked which single thing he found most evocative of Paris. The venerable logical positivist thought for a while, and then answered, 'A road sign with "Paris" written on it.'

Kettle

Some people lose their sense of proportion; I've lost my sense of scale. Arriving home from London late last night, I found myself unable to judge the distance from the last exit sign for Junction 4 to the slip road itself. Granted it was foggy and the bright headlights of oncoming vehicles burned expanding aureoles into my view, but there are three white-bordered, oblong signs, arranged sequentially to aid people like me.

The first has three oblique bars (set in blue); the second, two; and the third, one. By the time you draw level with the third sign you should have already begun to appreciate the meaning of the curved wedge, adumbrated with further oblique white lines, that forms an interzone, an unplace, between the slip road, as it pares away, and the inside carriageway of the motorway, which powers on towards the Chiltern scarp.

The three signs are the run-in strip to the beginning of the film; they are the flying fingers of the pit-crew boss as he counts down Mansell; they are the decline in rank (from sergeant, to corporal, to lance corporal) that indicates your demotion from the motorway. Furthermore, the ability to co-ordinate their sequence with the falling needles on the warmly glowing instrument panel of the car is a sound indication that you can intuitively apprehend three different scales at once (time, speed, distance), and that you are able to merge them effortlessly into the virtual reality that is motorway driving.

But for some obscure reason the Ministry has slipped up here. At the Beaconsfield exit there is far too long a gap between the last sign and the start of the slip road. I fell into this gap and lost my sense of scale. It occurred to me, when at last I gained the roundabout, and the homey, green sign (Beaconsfield 4) heaved into view, that this gap, this lacuna, was, in terms of my projected thesis, 'No Services: Reflex Ritualism and Modern Motorway Signs (with special reference to the

4 M40)' – an aspect of what the French call *délire*.

In other words that part of the text that is a deviation or derangement, not contained within the text, and yet defines the text better than the text itself.

I almost crashed. By the time I reached home (a modest bungalow set hard against the model village that is Beaconsfield's principal visitor attraction), I had just about stopped shaking. I went straight to the kitchen. The baking tray I had left in the oven that morning had become a miniature Death Valley of hard-baked morphine granules. The dark brown rime lay in a ruckled surface, broken here and there into regular patterns of scales, like the skin of some moribund lizard. I used a steel spatula to scrape the material up and placed it carefully in a small plastic bowl decorated with leaping bunnies. (After the divorce my wife organized the division of the chattels. She took all the adult-size plates and cutlery, leaving me with the diminutive ware that our children had outgrown.)

I have no formal training in chemistry, but somehow, by a process of hit and miss, I have developed a method whereby I can precipitate a soluble tartrate from raw morphine granules. The problem with the stuff is that it still contains an appreciable amount of chalk. This is because I obtain my supplies in the form of bottles of kaolin and morphine purchased in sundry chemists. If I leave the bottles to sit for long enough, most of the morphine rises to the top. But you can never eradicate all the kaolin, and when the morphine suspension is siphoned off, some of the kaolin invariably comes as well.

Months of injecting this stuff have given my body an odd aspect, as with every shot more chalk is deposited along the walls of my veins, much in the manner of earth being piled up to form either an embankment or a cutting around a roadway. Thus the history of my addiction has been mapped out by me, in the same way that the road system of South-East England was originally constructed.

To begin with, conscious of the effects, I methodically worked my way through the veins in my arms and legs, turning them first the tannish colour of drovers' paths, then the darker brown of cart tracks, until eventually they became macadamized, blackened, by my abuse. Finally I turned my attention to the arteries. Now, when I stand on the broken bathroom scales and contemplate my route-planning image in the full-length mirror, I see a network of calcified conduits radiating from my groin. Some of them are scored into my flesh like underpasses, others are raised up on hardened revetments of flesh: bloody flyovers.

I have been driven to using huge five-millilitre barrels, fitted with the long, blue-collared needles necessary for hitting arteries. I am very conscious that, should I miss, the consequences for my circulatory system could be disastrous. I might lose a limb and cause tailbacks right the way round the M25. Sometimes I wonder if I may be losing my incident room.

There's this matter of the thesis, to begin with. Not only is the subject matter obscure (some might say risible), but I have no grant or commission. It would be all right if I were some dilettante, privately endowed, who could afford to toy with such things, but I am not. Rather, I both have myself to support and have to keep up the maintenance. If the maintenance isn't kept up, my ex-wife – who is frequently levelled by spirits – will become as obdurate as any consulting civil engineer. She has it within her power to arrange bollards around me, or even to insist on the introduction of tolls to pay for the maintenance. There could be questions in the bungalow – something I cannot abide.

But last night none of this troubled me. I was lost in the arms of Morphia. As I pushed home the plunger she spoke to me thus: 'Left hand down. Harder . . . harder . . . harder!' And around I swept, pinned by g force into the tight circularity of history. In my reverie I saw the M40 as it will be some 20,000 years from now, when the second neolithic age has dawned over Europe.

Still no services. All six carriageways and the hard shoulder are grassed over. The long enfilades of dipping halogen lights, which used to wade in concrete, are gone, leaving behind shallow depressions visible from the air. Every single one of the distance markers 'Birmingham 86' has been crudely tipped to the horizontal, forming a series of steel biers. On top of them are the decomposing corpses of motorway chieftains, laid out for excarnation prior to interment. Their bones are to be

8

placed in chambers, mausoleums that have been hollowed out from the gigantic concrete caissons of moribund motorway bridges.

I was conscious of being one of these chieftains, these princelings of the thoroughfare. And as I stared up into the dark, dark blue of a sky that was near to the end of history, I was visited by a horrible sense of claustrophobia – the claustrophobia that can come only when no space is great enough to contain you, not the involution that is time itself.

I have no idea how long I must have lain there, observing the daily life of the simple motorway folk, but it was long enough for me to gain an appreciation of the subtlety with which they had adapted this monumental ruin. While the flat expanse of the carriageways was used for rudimentary agriculture, the steeply raked embankments were left for aurochs, moufflon and other newly primitive grazers.

The motorway tribe was divided up into clans or extended families, each of which had made its encampment at a particular junction and taken a different item of the prehistoric road furniture for its totem. My clan – Junction 2, that is – had somehow managed to preserve a set of cat's eyes from the oblivion of time. These were being worn by the chieftain, bound into his complicated headdress, when he came to see how I was getting on with decomposing.

'You must understand,' he said, observing the Star Trek convention, whereby even the most outlandish peoples still speak standard English, 'that we view the M40 as a giant astronomical clock. We use the slip roads, maintenance areas, bridges and flyovers azimuthally, to predict the solstices and hence the seasons. Ours is a religion both of great antiquity and of a complexity that belies our simple agrarian culture. Although we are no longer able to read or write ourselves, our priesthood has orally transmitted down the genera-. tions the sacred revelations contained in this ancient text.' With this he produced from a fold in his cloak a copy of 'No Services: Reflex Ritualism and Modern Motorway Signs (with special reference to the M40)', my as yet unwritten thesis.

Needless to say, this uncharacteristically upbeat ending to my narcotic vision left me feeling more melioristic than usual when I awoke this morning. Staggering to the kitchen I snapped on the radio. A disc jockey ululated an intro while I put on the kettle. The sun was rising over the model village. From where I sat I could see its rays reflected by a thousand tiny diamond-patterned windows. I sipped my tea; it tasted flat, as listless as myself. Looking into the cup I could see that the brown fluid was supporting an archipelago of scale. Dirty grey-brown stuff, tattered and variegated. I went back to the kitchen and peered into the kettle. Not only was the interior almost completely choked by scale, but the descaler itself was furred over, transformed into a chrysalis by mineral deposits. I resolved that today I would visit the ironmonger's and purchase a new descaler.

It's on my route – the ironmonger's – for I've burnt down every chemist in Beaconsfield in the last few months, and now I must head further afield for my kaolin and morphine supplies. I must voyage to Tring, to Amersham and even up the M40, to High Wycombe.

Relative

'Can I pay for these?'

'Whassat?'

'Can I pay for these – these descalers?' Time is standing still in the ironmonger's. Outside, a red-and-white-striped awning protects an array of brightly coloured washing-up bowls from the drizzle. Inside, the darkness is scented with nails and resinous timber. I had no idea that the transaction would prove so gruelling. The proprietor of the ironmonger's is looking at me the same way that the pharmacist does when I go to buy my kaolin and morphine.

'Why d'you want three?' Is it my imagination, or does his voice really have an edge of suspicion? What does he suspect me of? Some foul and unnatural practice carried out with kettle descalers? It hardly seems likely.

'I've got an incredible amount of scale in my

kettle, that's why.' I muster an insouciance I simply don't feel. Since I have been accused, I know that I am guilty. I know that I lure young children away from the precincts of the model village and subject them to appalling, brutal, inter-crural sex. I abrade their armpits, their kneepits, the junctures of their thighs, with my spun mini-rolls of wire. That's why I need three.

Guilt dogs me as I struggle to ascend the high street, stepping on the heels of my shoes, almost tripping me up. Guilt about my children – that's the explanation for the scene in the ironmonger's. Ever since my loss of sense of scale, I have found it difficult to relate to my children. They no longer feel comfortable coming to visit me here in Beaconsfield. They say they would rather stay with their mother. The model village, which used to entrance them, now bores them.

Perhaps it was an indulgence on my part – moving to a bungalow next to the model village. It's true that when I sat, puffing on my pipe, watching my son and daughter move about amongst the four-foot-high, half-timbered semis, I would feel transported, taken back to my own childhood. It was the confusion in scale that allowed this. For if the model village was to scale, my children would be at least sixty feet tall. Easily big enough, and competent enough, to re-parent me.

It was the boy who blew the whistle on me, grassed me up to his mother. At seven, he is old enough to know the difference between the smell of tobacco and the smell that comes from my pipe. Naturally he told his mother and she realized immediately that I was back on the M.

In a way I don't blame him – it's a filthy habit. And the business of siphoning off the morphine from the bottles and then baking it in the oven until it forms a smokable paste. Well I mean, it's pathetic, this DIY addiction. No wonder that there are no pleasure domes for me, in my *bricolage* reverie. Instead I see twice five yards of fertile ground, with sheds and raspberry canes girded round. In a word: an allotment.

When my father died he subdivided his allotment and left a fifth of it to each of his children. The Association wouldn't allow it. They said that allotments were only leased rather than owned. It's a great pity, because what with the subsidies available and the new intensive agricultural methods, I could probably have made a reasonable living out of my fifth. I can just see myself . . . making hay with a kitchen fork, spreading silage with a teaspoon, bringing in the harvest with a wheelbarrow, ploughing with a trowel tied to a two-by-four. Bonsai cattle wind o'er the lea of the compost heap as I recline in the pet cemetery.

It was not to be.

Returning home from High Wycombe I add the contents of my two new bottles of kaolin and morphine to the plant. Other people have ginger-beer plants; I have a morphine plant. I made my morphine plant out of a plastic sterilizing unit. It would be a nice irony, this transmogrification of taboo, were it not for the fact that every time I clap eyes on the thing I remember with startling accuracy what it looked like full of teats and bottles, when the children were babies and I was a happier man. I think I mentioned the division of chattels following the divorce. This explains why I ended up, here in Beaconsfield, with the decorative Tupperware, the baby-bouncer, sundry activity centres and the aforementioned sterilizing unit.

Whereas my ex-wife resides in St John's Wood, reclining on an emperor-size bateau-lit. When I cast off and head out on to the sea of sleep my vessel is a plastic changing mat, patterned with Fred Flintstones and Barney Rubbles.

It's lucky for me that the five 'police procedurals' I wrote during my marriage are still selling well. Without the royalties I don't think I would be able to keep my family in the manner to which they have unfortunately become accustomed. I cannot imagine that the book I am currently working on, *Murder on the Median Strip*, will do a fraction as well. (I say that confidently, but what fraction do I mean? Certainly not a half or a quarter, but why not a fiftieth or a hundredth? This is certainly conceivable. I must try and be more accurate with my figures of speech. I must use them as steel rulers to delimit thought. Woolliness will be my undoing.)

In *Murder on the Median Strip* (henceforth M *on the MS*), a young woman is raped, murdered and buried on the median strip of the M40 in between Junction 2 (Beaconsfield) and Junction 3 (High Wycombe). As shall become apparent, it is a howdunnit, rather than a whodunnit. The murder occurs late on a Friday evening when the motorway is still crowded with ex-urbanites heading for home. The police are patrolling, looking for speeders. Indeed, they have set up a radar trap between the two principal bridges on this section of road. And yet no one notices anything.

When the shallow, bitumen-encrusted grave is discovered, the police, indulging in their penchant for overkill, decide to reconstruct the entire incident. They put out a call on *Crimewatch UK* for all those who were on the motorway in that place, at that time, to reassemble at Junction 2. The public response is overwhelming, and by virtue of careful interviewing – the recollection of number plates, makes of car, children making faces and so forth – they establish that they have managed to net all the cars and drivers that could have been there. The logistics of this are immensely complicated. But such is the ghastliness of the crime that the public demands that the resources be expended. Eventually, by dint of computer-aided visualizations, the police are able to re-enact the whole incident. The cars set off at intervals; the police hover overhead in helicopters; officers in patrol cars and on foot question any passers-by. But, horror of horrors, while the reconstruction is actually taking place, the killer strikes again – this time between Junction 6 (Watlington) and Junction 7 (Thame). Once more his victim is a young woman, whom he sexually assaults, strangles, and then crudely inters beneath the static steel fender of the crash barrier.

That's as far as I've got with *M on the MS*. Sometimes, contemplating the MS, I begin to feel that I've painted myself into a corner with this convoluted plot. I realize that I may have tried to stretch the credulity of my potential readers too far.

In a way the difficulties of the plot mirror my own difficulties as a writer. In creating such an unworkable and fantastic scenario I have managed, at least, to fulfil my father's expectations of my craft.

'There's no sense of scale in your books,' he said to me shortly before he died. At that time I had written only two procedurals, both featuring Inspector Archimedes, my idiosyncratic Greek

Cypriot detective. 'You can have a limited success,' he went on, 'chipping away like this at the edges of society, chiselling off microscopic fragments of observation. But really important writing provides some sense of the relation between individual psychology and social change, of the scale of things in general. You can see that if you look at the great nineteenth-century novels.' He puffed on his pipe as he spoke, and, observing his wrinkled, scaly hide and the way his red lips and yellow teeth masticated the black stem, I was reminded of a basking lizard, sticking its tongue out at the world.

A letter came this morning from the Municipality, demanding payment of their property tax. When I first moved here, a man came from the borough valuer's to assess the rateable value of the bungalow. I did some quick work with the trellises and managed to make it look as if Number 59, Crendon Road, was in fact one of the houses in the model village.

To begin with, the official disputed the idea that I could possibly be living in this pocket-sized dwelling, but I managed to convince him that I was a doctoral student writing a thesis on 'The Apprehension of Scale in *Gulliver's Travels*, with special reference to Lilliput', and that the operators of the model village had leased the house to me so that I could gain first-hand experience of Gulliver's state of mind. I even entered the house and adopted some attitudes – head on the kitchen table, left leg rammed through the french windows – in order to persuade him.

The result of this clever charade was that for two years my rates were assessed on the basis of 7ft 8in sq. of living space. I had to pay £11.59 per annum. Now, of course, I am subject to the full whack. Terribly unfair. And anyway, if the tax is determined by the individual rather than by the property, what if that individual has a hazy or distorted sense of self? Shouldn't people with acute dissociation, or multiple personalities, be forced to pay more? I have resolved not to pay the tax until I have received a visit from the borough clinical psychologist.

The Ascent

'Affected as well as asinine', *TLS*

Some of my innovations regarding the new genre of 'Motorway Verse' have been poorly received, both by the critics and by the reading public. My claim, that what my motorway verse is trying to do represents a return to the very roots of *poetas*, an inspired attempt to link modish hermeneutics to the original function of oral literature, has been dismissed *sans phrase*.

I myself cannot even understand the thrust of this criticism. It seems to me self-evident that the subconscious apprehension of signs by motorway drivers is exactly analogous to that act whereby the poets of primitive cultures give life, actually breathe reality into the land.

Taking the M40 as an example of this:

> Jnctn 1. Uxbridge. Jnctn 1A. (M25) M4.
> Jnctn 2. Slough A365. No Services.
> On M40 . . .

would be a very believable sample of such a 'signing up' of the country. Naturally, in order to understand the somewhat unusual scansion, it is necessary that readers imaginatively place themselves in a figurative car that is actually driving up the aforementioned motorway. Metrical feet are, therefore, to be determined as much by feeling through the pedals the shift from macadamized to concrete surfaces, and by hearing the susurration produced by alterations in the height and material construction of the crash barrier, as by the rhythm of the words themselves.

Furthermore, a motorway verse that attempts to describe the ascent of the Chiltern scarp from the Oxfordshire side will, of course, be profoundly different to one that chronicles the descent from Junction 5 (Stokenchurch) to Junction 6 (Watlington). For example:

> Crawling, crawling, crawling. Crawler Lane
> Slow-slow O'Lorry-o. Lewknor. 50 mph max.
> 11T! Narrow lanes, narrowing, narr-o-wing,
>   na-rro-wing.

24   as opposed to:

F'tum. F'tum. F'tum.
Kerchunk, kerchunk (Wat–ling–ton) . . .

Well, I'm certain no one reading this had any difficulty in divining which was which!

On the Continent they are not afflicted by the resistance to the modern that so entirely characterizes English cultural life. In France, '*Vers Péage*' is a well-respected genre, already making its way on to university syllabuses. Indeed I understand that a critical work is soon to be published that concerns itself solely with the semantic incongruities presented by the term 'soft verge'.

It has occurred to me that it could be my introduction of motorway symbology itself, as if it were an extension of the conventional alphabet, that has hardened the hearts of these penny-ante time-servers, possessors of tenure (but no grip), and the like. But it seems to me that the white arrow pointing down, obliquely, to the right; the ubiquitous '11T' lane-closing ideogram; the emotive, omega-like, overhead '[X]'; and many many others all have an equal right to be considered capable of meaningful combination with orthodox characters.

On bad days, days when the tedium and obscurity of my life here at Beaconsfield seem almost justified, I am embarrassed to say that I console myself with the thought that there may be some grand conspiracy, taking in critics, publishers, editors and the executives in charge of giant typefounders such as Monotype, to stop my verse from gaining any success. For, were it to do so, they would have to alter radically the range of typefaces that they provide.

Is it any wonder that I look for consolation – partly in draughts of sickly morphine syrup (drunk straight off the top of bottles of kaolin and morphine), and partly in hard, dedicated work on my motorway saga, entitled *From Birmingham to London and Back Again Delivering Office Equipment, with Nary a Service Centre to Break the Monotony*?

There's that, and there's also the carving of netsuke, at which I am becoming something of an expert. I have chosen to concentrate on rendering in ivory the monumental works of modern sculptors. Thus, I have now completed a set of early Caros and Henry Moores, all of which could be comfortably housed in a pup tent.

The ebb and flow of my opiate addiction is something that I have come to prize as a source of literary inspiration. When I am beginning a new habit, my hypnagogic visions are intricate processions of images that I can both summon and manipulate at will. But when I am withdrawing, I am frequently plunged into startling nightmares. Nightmares that seem to last for eons and yet of which I am conscious – at one and the same time – as taking place within a single REM.

Last night's dream was a classic case of this clucking phenomenon. In it, I found myself leaving the bungalow and entering the precincts of the model village. I wandered around the forty-foot-long village green, admiring the precision and attention to detail that the model makers have lavished on their creation. I peeked first into the model butcher's shop. Lilliputian rashers of bacon were laid out on plastic trays, together with sausages, perfect in every respect, but the size of mouse droppings. Then I sauntered over to the post office. On the eight-inch-high counter sat an envelope the size of a postage stamp. Wonder of wonders, I could even read the address on the envelope. It was a poll-tax demand, destined for me.

Straightening up abruptly I caught sight of two model buildings that I was unfamiliar with. The first of these was a small, but perfectly formed, art gallery. Looking through the tall windows I could see, inside, on the polished wooden floor, a selection of my netsuke. The Caros rather than the Moores. Preposterous, I thought to myself, with one of those leaps of dream logic; a real village of this size would never have an art gallery. Let alone one exhibiting the works of an internationally renowned sculptor.

The second building was my own bungalow. I couldn't be certain of this – it is after all not that remarkable an edifice – until I had looked in through the kitchen window. There, under the dirty cream melamine work surface surrounding the aluminium sink, I could see hundreds of little kaolin and morphine bottles, serried in dusty ranks. That settled it.

As soon as I had clapped eyes on them, I found myself miraculously reduced in size and able to enter the model bungalow. I wandered from room to room, more than a little discomfited at my phantasmagoric absorption into Beaconsfield's premier visitor attraction. Stepping on to the sun porch I found another model – as it were, a model model. Also of the bungalow. Once again I was diminished and able to enter.

I must have gone through at least four more of these vertiginous descents in scale before I was able to stop, and think, and prevent myself from examining another model bungalow. As it was I knew that I must be standing in a sun porch for which a double-glazing estimate would have to be calculated in angstroms. From the position I found myself in, to be 002 scale would have been, to me, gargantuan. How to get back? That was the problem.

It is fortunate indeed that in my youth I spent many hours tackling the more difficult climbs around Wastdale Head. These rocky scrambles, although close to the tourist tramps up the peaks of Scafell Pike and Helvellyn, are nevertheless amongst the most demanding rock climbs in Europe.

It took me three months to ascend, back up the six separate stages of scale, and reach home once more. Some of the pitches, especially those involving climbing down off the various tables the model bungalows were placed on, I would wager were easily the most extreme ever attempted by a solo climber. On many occasions, I found myself dangling from the rope I had plaited out of strands of carpet underlay, with no apparent way of regaining the slick varnished face of the table leg, and the checkerboard of lino – relative to my actual size – some six hundred feet below.

Oh, the stories I could tell! The sights I saw! It would need an epic to contain them. As it is I have restrained myself – although, on awakening, I did write a letter to the Alpine Club on the ethics of climbers, finding themselves in such situations, using paper clips as fixed crampons.

The final march across the 'true' model village to my bungalow was, of course, the most frightening. When contained within the Russian-doll series of ever diminishing bungalows, I had been aware that the ordinary laws of nature were, to some extent, in abeyance. However, out in the village I knew that I was exposed to all the familiar terrors of small-scale adventuring: wasps the size of zeppelins, fluff-falls the weight of an avalanche, mortar-bomb explosions of plant spore, and so on and so forth.

My most acute anxiety, as I traversed the model village, was that I would be sighted by a human. I was aware that I could not be much larger than a sub-atomic particle, and as such I would be subject to Heisenberg's Uncertainty Principle. Were I to be in any way observed, not only might I find the direction of my journey irremediably altered, I could even cease to exist altogether!

It happened as I picked my way over the first of the steps leading up from the village to my bungalow. The very grain of the concrete formed a lunar landscape which I knew would take me days to journey across. I wiped the sweat that dripped from my sunburnt brow. Something vast, inconceivably huge, was moving up ahead of me. It was a man! To scale! He turned, and his turning was like some geological event, the erosion of a mountain range or the undulation of the Mohorovicic Discontinuity itself!

It was one of the maintenance men who works in the model village. I knew it because, emblazoned across the back of his blue boiler suit, picked out in white as on a motorway sign, was the single word 'MAINTENANCE'. His giant eye loomed towards me, growing bigger and bigger, until the red-and-blue veins that snaked across the bilious ball were as the Orinoco or the Amazon, to my petrified gaze. He blinked – and I winked out of existence.

I don't need to tell you that when I awoke sweating profusely, the covers twisted around my quaking body like a strait-jacket, I had no difficulty at all in interpreting the dream.

To the Bathroom

'Like, we're considering the historic present –?'

'Yeah.'

'And David says, "I want to go to the bathroom."'

'Yeah.'

'So, like we all accompany him there and stuff. 'Cos in his condition it wouldn't like be a . . . be a –'

'Good idea for him to be alone?'

'Yeah, thassit. So we're standing there, right. All four of us, in the bathroom, and David's doing what he has to do. And we're still talking about it.'

'It?'

'The historic present. Because Diane – you know Diane?'

'Sort of.'

'Well, she says the historic present is, like . . .

er . . . like, more emotionally labile than other tenses. Yeah, thass what she says. Anyways, she's saying this and David is, like, steaming, man . . . I mean to say he's really plummeting. It's like he's being de-cored or something. This isn't just Montezuma's revenge, it's everyone's revenge. It's the revenge of every deracinated group of indigenes ever to have had the misfortune to encounter the European. It's a sort of collective curse of David's colon. It's like his colon is being crucified or something.'

'He's anally labile.'

'Whadjewsay?'

'He's anally labile.'

Labile, labile. Labby lips. Libby-labby lips. This is the kind of drivel I've been reduced to. Imaginary dialogues between myself and a non-existent interlocutor. But is it any surprise? I mean to say, if you have a colon as spastic as mine it's bound to insinuate itself into every aspect of your thinking. My trouble is I'm damned if I do and I'm damned if I don't. If I don't drink vast quantities of kaolin and morphine I'm afflicted with the most terrifying bouts of diarrhoea. And if I do – drink a couple of bottles a day, that is – I'm subject to the most appalling undulations, seismic colonic ructions. It doesn't really stop the shits either. I still get them, I just don't get caught short. Caught short on the hard shoulder, that's the killer.

Say you're driving up to High Wycombe, for example. Just out on a commonplace enough errand. Like going to buy a couple of bottles of K&M. And you're swooping down towards Junction 3, the six lanes of blacktop twisting away from you like some colossal wastepipe, through which the automotive crap of the metropolis is being voided into the rural septic tank, when all of a sudden you're overcome. You pull over on to the hard shoulder, get out of the car, and squat down. Hardly dignified. And not only that, destructive of the motorway itself. Destructive of the purity of one's recollection.

That's why I prefer to stay home in my kaolin-lined bungalow. I prefer to summon up my memories of the motorway in the days before I was so afflicted. In the days when my vast *roman-fleuve* was barely a trickle, and my sense of scale was 35 intact. Then, distance was defined by regular increments, rather than by the haphazard lurch from movement to movement.

This morning I was sitting, not really writing, just dabbling. I was hunkered down inside myself, my ears unconsciously registering the whisper, whistle and whicker of the traffic on the M40, when I got that sinking feeling. I hied me to the bathroom, just in time to see a lanky youth disappearing out of the window, with my bathroom scales tucked under his arm.

I grabbed a handful of his hip-length jacket and pulled him back into the room. He was a mangy specimen. His head was badly shaven, with spirals of ringworm on the pitted surface. The youth had had these embellished with crude tattoos, as if to dignify his repulsive skin condition. His attire was a loose amalgam of counter-cultural styles, the ragged chic of a redundant generation. His pupils were so dilated that the black was getting on to his face. I instantly realized that I had nothing to fear from him. He didn't cry out, or even attempt to struggle.

36   I had seen others like him. There's quite a

posse of them, these 'model heads'. That's what they call themselves. They congregate around the model village, venerating it as a symbol of their anomie. It's as if, by becoming absorbed in the detail of this tiny world, they hope to diminish the scale of society's problems. In the winter they go abroad, settling near Legoland in Belgium.

'Right, you,' I said, in householder tones. 'You might have thought that you'd get away with nicking something as trivial as those bathroom scales, but it just so happens that they have a sentimental value for me.'

'Whadjergonna do then?' He was bemused – not belligerent.

'I'm going to put you on trial, that's what I'm going to do.'

'You're not gonna call the filth, are you?'

'No, no. No need. In Beaconsfield we have extended the whole principle of Neighbourhood Watch to include the idea of neighbourhood justice. I will sit in judgment on you myself. If you wish, my court will appoint a lawyer who will organize your defence.'

'Err –' He had slumped down on top of the 37

wicker laundry basket, which made him look even more like one of Ali Baba's anorectic confrères. 'Yeah, OK, whatever you say.'

'Good. I will represent you myself. Allow me, if you will, to assume my position on the bench.' We shuffled around each other in the confinement of tiles. I put the seat down, sat down, and said, 'The court may be seated.'

For a while after that nothing happened. The two of us sat in silence, listening to the rising and falling flute of the Vent-Axia. I thought about the day the court-appointed officer had come to deliver my decree nisi. He must have been reading the documents in the car as he drove up the motorway, because when I encountered him on the doorstep he was trying hard – but failing – to suppress a smirk of amusement.

I knew why. My wife had sued for divorce on the grounds of adultery. The co-respondent was known to her, and the place where the adultery had taken place was none other than on these selfsame scales. The ones the model head had just attempted to steal. At that time they were still located in the bathroom of our London house.

After the decree absolute, my ex-wife sent them to me in Beaconsfield, together with a caustic note.

It was a hot summer afternoon in the bathroom. I was with a lithe young foreign woman, who was full of capricious lust. 'Come on,' she said, 'let's do it on the scales. It'll be fun, we'll look like some weird astrological symbol, or a diagram from the *Kama Sutra*.' She twisted out of her dress and pulled off her underwear. I stood on the scales. Even translated from metric to imperial measure, my bodyweight still looked unimpressive. She hooked her hands around my neck and jumped. The flanges of flesh on the inside of her thighs neatly fitted the notches above my bony hips. I grasped the fruit of her buttocks in my sweating palms. She braced herself, feet against the wall, toenails snagging on the Artex. Her panting smoked the mirror on the medicine cabinet. I moved inside her. The coiled spring inside the scales squeaked and groaned. Eventually it broke altogether.

That's how my wife twigged. When she next went to weigh herself she found the scales jammed, the pointer registering 322 lb. Exactly the combined weight of me and the family *au pair* . . .

Oh, *mene, mene, tekel, upharsin*! What a fool I was! Now fiery hands retributively mangle my innards! The demons play upon my sackbut and I am cast into the fiery furnace of evacuation. I am hooked there, a toilet duck, condemned for ever to lick under the rim of life!

The model head snapped me out of my fugue. 'You're a Libra,' he said, 'aren't you?'

'Whassat?'

'Your sign. It's Libra, innit?' He was regarding me with the preternatural stare of a madman or a seer.

'Well, yes, as a matter of fact, it is.'

'I'm good at that. Guessing people's astrological signs. Libras are, like, er . . . creative an' that.'

'I s'pose so.'

'But they also find it hard to come to decisions –'

'Are you challenging the authority of this court?' I tried to sound magisterial, but realized that the figure I cut was ridiculous.

'Nah, nah. I wouldn't do that, mate. It's just . . . like I mean to say, whass the point, an' that?'

I couldn't help but agree with him, so I let him go. I even insisted that he take the bathroom scales with him. After all, what good are they to me now?

Lizard

Epilogue. Many years later . . .

If you want to walk round the Lizard Peninsula, you have to be reasonably well equipped. Which is not to say that this part of Cornwall is either particularly remote (the M5 now goes all the way to Land's End) or that rugged. It's just that the exposure to so much wind and sky, and so many pasties, after a winter spent huddled on the urban periphery (somewhere like Beaconsfield, for example), can have an unsettling effect. I always advise people to take an antacid preparation, and also some kaolin and morphine. There's no need any more to carry an entire bottle, for Sterling Health have thoughtfully created a tablet form of this basic but indispensable remedy.

One other word of warning before you set out. Don't be deceived by the map into thinking that distances of, say, eight to ten miles represent a comfortable afternoon's stroll. The Lizard is so

43

called because of the many rocky inlets that are gouged out of its scaly sides, giving the entire landmass the aspect of some giant creature, bound for the Atlantic vivarium. The coastal path is constantly either ascending or descending around these inlets. Therefore, to gain a mile you may have to go up and down as much as six hundred feet.

I myself haven't been to the Lizard for many years, in fact not since I was a young man. Even if I felt strong enough to make the journey now, I wouldn't go. For those younger than I, who cannot remember a time before the current Nationalist Trust Government took power, the prospect may still seem inviting. But personally, I find that the thought of encountering the Government's Brown Shirts, with their oak-leaf epaulettes, sticks in my craw. I would bitterly resent being compelled by these paramilitary nature wardens to admire the scenery, register the presence (or even absence) of ancient monuments, and propitiate the wayside waste shrines with crumpled offerings.

Of course, we aren't altogether immune from the depredations of the Trust here in Beaconsfield.

Last month, after a bitterly fought local election, they gained power in almost all of the wards, including the one that contains the model village itself. There have been rumours, discreet mutterings, that they intend to introduce their ubiquitous signs to the village. These will designate parts of it areas of (albeit minute) 'outstanding natural beauty'.

But I am old now, and have not the stomach for political infighting. Since the publication of the last volume of my magnum opus, *A History of the English Motorway Service Centre*, I have gained a modest eminence. People tell me that I am referred to as 'the Macaulay of the M40', a sobriquet that, I must confess, gives me no little pleasure. I feel vindicated by the verdict of posterity. (I say posterity, for I am now so old that hardly anyone realizes I am still alive.)

I spend most of my days out on the sun porch. Here I lie naked, for all the world like some moribund reptile, sopping up the rays. My skin has turned mahogany with age and melanoma. It's difficult for me to distinguish now between the daub of cancerous sarcoma and the toughened wattle of my flesh. Be that as it may, I am not frightened of death. I feel no pain, despite having long since reduced the indulgence of my pernicious habituation to kaolin and morphine to a mere teaspoonful every hour.

With age have come stoicism and repose. When I was younger I could not focus on anything, or even apprehend a single thought, without feeling driven to incorporate it into some architectonic, some Great Design. I was also plagued by lusts, both fleshly and demonic, which sent me into such dizzying spirals of self-negation that I was compelled to narcosis.

But now, even the contemplation of the most trivial things can provide enough sensual fodder to last me an entire morning. Today, for example, I became transfixed, staring into the kettle, by the three separate levels of scale therein. First the tangible scale, capping the inverted cradle of the water's meniscus. Secondly, the crystalline accretions of scale that wreathed the element. And thirdly, of course, the very abstract notion of 'scale' itself, implied by my unreasoned observation. It's as if I were possessed of some kind of

Escher-vision, allowing me constantly to perceive the dimensional conundrum that perception presents.

I am also comforted in my solitude by my pets. One beneficial side-effect of the change in climate has been the introduction of more exotic species to this isle. But whereas the *nouveaux riches* opt for the Pantagruelian spectacle of giraffes cropping their laburnums, and hippopotamuses wallowing in their sun-saturated swimming pools, I have chosen to domesticate the more elegant frill-necked lizard.

This curious reptile, with its preposterous vermilion ruff, stands erect on its hind legs like a miniature dinosaur. When evening comes, and the day's visitors have departed, I let it out so that it may roam the lanes and paths of the model village. The sight of this pocket Godzilla stalking the dwarfish environs, its head darting this way and that, as if on the look-out for a canapé-sized human, never fails to amuse me.

However, not every aspect of my life is quite so easeful and reposed. The occasional dispute, relating to a lifetime of scholarly endeavour, still flares up occasionally. It is true that my work has a certain status here in England, but of course all this means in practice is that although many have heard of it, few have actually read any of it.

In the ex-colonies the situation is different. A Professor Moi wrote to me last year, from the University of Uganda, to dispute the findings of my seminal paper 'When is a Road Not a Road?',* in which – if you can be bothered to recall – I established a theory that a motorway cannot be said to be a motorway unless it is longer than it is broad. I was inspired to this by my contemplation of the much maligned A41(M), which at that time ran for barely a mile. Moi took issue with the theory, and after I had perused the relevant Ugandan gazetteer it became clear to me why.

The ill-fated Lusaka Bypass was to have been the centrepiece of the Ugandan Government's Motorway Construction Programme. However, resources ran out after only one junction and some eighty feet of road had been built. Faced with the options of either changing the nomenclature or

* British Journal of Ephemera, Spring 1986

admitting failure, the Ugandans had no alternative but to take issue with the theory itself.

But such episodes are infrequent. Mostly I am left alone by the world. My children have grown up and disappointed me; my former friends and acquaintances have forgotten me. If I do receive any visitors nowadays, they are likely to be young professional couples, nascent ex-urbanites, come to enquire whether or not the bungalow is for sale.

It is a delicious irony that although when I first moved to Beaconsfield the bungalow was regarded as tacky in the extreme, over the years it has become a period piece. The aluminium-framed picture windows, the pebbledash façade, the corrugated-perspex carport: all of these are now regarded as delightfully authentic and original features. Such is the queer humour of history.

And what of the M40 itself, the fount of my life's work? How stands it? Well, I must confess that since the universal introduction of electric cars with a maximum speed of 15 mph, the glamour of motorway driving seems entirely lost. Every so often I'll take the golf buggy out and tootle up towards Junction 5 (Stokenchurch), but my motives are really rather morbid.

Morbid, for it is here that I am to be buried. Here, where the motorway plunges through a gunsight cutting and the rolling plain of Oxfordshire spreads out into the blue distance. Just beyond the Chiltern scarp the M40 bisects the Ridgeway, that neolithic drovers' path which was the motorway of Stone Age Britain. It is here that the Nationalist Trust has given gracious permission for me to construct my mausoleum.

I have opted for something in the manner of an ancient chamber tomb. A long, regular heap of layered stones, with corbelled walls rising to a slab roof. At one end the burial mound will tastefully elide with the caisson of the bridge on which the M40 spans the Ridgeway.

It is a fitting memorial, and what's more, I am convinced that it will remain long after the motorway itself has become little more than a grassed-over ruin, a monument to a dead culture. The idea that perhaps, in some distant future, disputatious archaeologists will find themselves flummoxed by the discovery of my tomb, together with its midden of discarded motorway signs, brings a twitch to my jowls.

Will the similarities in construction between my tomb and the great chamber tombs of Ireland and the Orkneys lead them to posit a continuous motorway culture, lasting some 7,000 years? I hope so. It has always been my contention that phenomena such as Silbury Hill and the Avebury stone circle can best be understood as, respectively, an embankment and a roundabout.

And so it seems that it is only by taking this very, very, long-term view that the answer to that pernicious riddle 'Why are there no services on the M40?' will find an answer.

In conclusion, then. It may be said of me that I have lost my sense of scale, but never that I have lost my sense of proportion.

PENGUIN 60s

PENGUIN 60s

READ MORE IN PENGUIN

For complete information about books available from Penguin and how to order them, please write to us at the appropriate address below. Please note that for copyright reasons the selection of books varies from country to country.

IN THE UNITED KINGDOM: Please write to *Dept. JC, Penguin Books Ltd, FREEPOST, West Drayton, Middlesex UB7 0BR.*
If you have any difficulty in obtaining a title, please send your order with the correct money, plus ten per cent for postage and packaging, to *PO Box No. 11, West Drayton, Middlesex UB7 0BR.*

IN THE UNITED STATES: Please write to *Consumer Sales, Penguin USA, P.O. Box 999, Dept. 17109, Bergenfield, New Jersey 07621-0120.* VISA and MasterCard holders call 1-800-253-6476 to order all Penguin titles.

IN CANADA: Please write to *Penguin Books Canada Ltd, 10 Alcorn Avenue, Suite 300, Toronto, Ontario M4V 3B2.*

IN AUSTRALIA: Please write to *Penguin Books Australia Ltd, P.O. Box 257, Ringwood, Victoria 3134.*

IN NEW ZEALAND: Please write to *Penguin Books (NZ) Ltd, Private Bag 102902, North Shore Mail Centre, Auckland 10.*

IN INDIA: Please write to *Penguin Books India Pvt Ltd, 706 Eros Apartments, 56 Nehru Place, New Delhi 110 019.*

IN THE NETHERLANDS: Please write to *Penguin Books Netherlands bv, Postbus 3507, NL-1001 AH Amsterdam.*

IN GERMANY: Please write to *Penguin Books Deutschland GmbH, Metzlerstrasse 26, 60594 Frankfurt am Main.*

IN SPAIN: Please write to *Penguin Books S. A., Bravo Murillo 19, 1o B, 28015 Madrid.*

IN ITALY: Please write to *Penguin Italia s.r.l., Via Felice Casati 20, I-20124 Milano.*

IN FRANCE: Please write to *Penguin France S. A., 17 rue Lejeune, F-31000 Toulouse.*

IN JAPAN: Please write to *Penguin Books Japan, Ishikiribashi Building, 2-5-4, Suido, Bunkyo-ku, Tokyo 112.*

IN GREECE: Please write to *Penguin Hellas Ltd, Dimocritou 3, GR-106 71 Athens.*

IN SOUTH AFRICA: Please write to *Longman Penguin Southern Africa (Pty) Ltd, Private Bag X08, Bertsham 2013.*